Zoom In on
Our Renewable Earth

Conservation

Andrea Rivera

abdopublishing.com

Published by Abdo Zoom™, PO Box 398166, Minneapolis, Minnesota 55439. Copyright © 2017 by Abdo Consulting Group, Inc. International copyrights reserved in all countries. No part of this book may be reproduced in any form without written permission from the publisher. Abdo Zoom™ is a trademark and logo of Abdo Consulting Group, Inc.

Printed in the United States of America, North Mankato, Minnesota
102016
012017

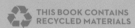

Cover Photo: Shutterstock Images
Interior Photos: Shutterstock Images, 1, 5, 11, 13, 14, 19, 21; Borut Trdina/iStockphoto, 4–5;
Riccardo Mayer/Shutterstock Images, 6; Christopher Futcher/iStockphoto, 7;
Ezume Images/Shutterstock Images, 8–9; Hurst Photo/Shutterstock Images, 10;
LP2 Studio/Shutterstock Images, 12; Aurore Marechal/Sipa USA/AP Images, 15;
Africa Studio/Shutterstock Images, 17; Mosay May/Shutterstock Images, 18

Editor: Emily Temple
Series Designer: Madeline Berger
Art Direction: Dorothy Toth

Publisher's Cataloging-in-Publication Data
Names: Rivera, Andrea, author.
Title: Conservation / by Andrea Rivera.
Description: Minneapolis, MN : Abdo Zoom, 2017. | Series: Our renewable Earth |
    Includes bibliographical references and index.
Identifiers: LCCN 2016948924 | ISBN 9781680799385 (lib. bdg.) |
    ISBN 9781624025242 (ebook) | ISBN 9781624025808 (Read-to-me ebook)
Subjects: LCSH: | Conservation of natural resources--Juvenile literature. |
    Renewable energy sources--Juvenile literature.
Classification: DDC 333.72--dc23
LC record available at http://lccn.loc.gov/2016948924

Table of Contents

Science 4

Technology. 8

Engineering 12

Art 14

Math 16

Key Stats. 20

Glossary 22

Booklinks 23

Index 24

Science

Earth has many natural resources.

But they are limited.

It is important not to
use them up.

Protecting them is called conservation.

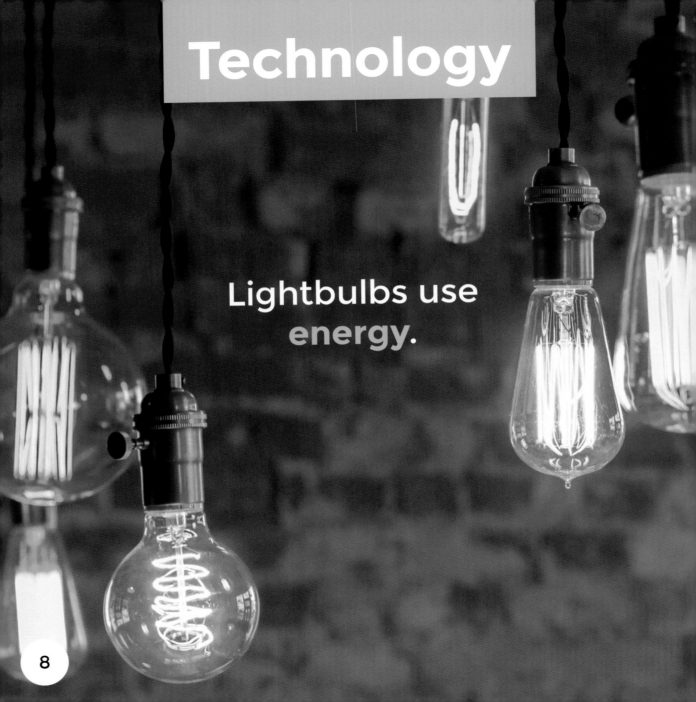

Technology

Lightbulbs use energy.

8

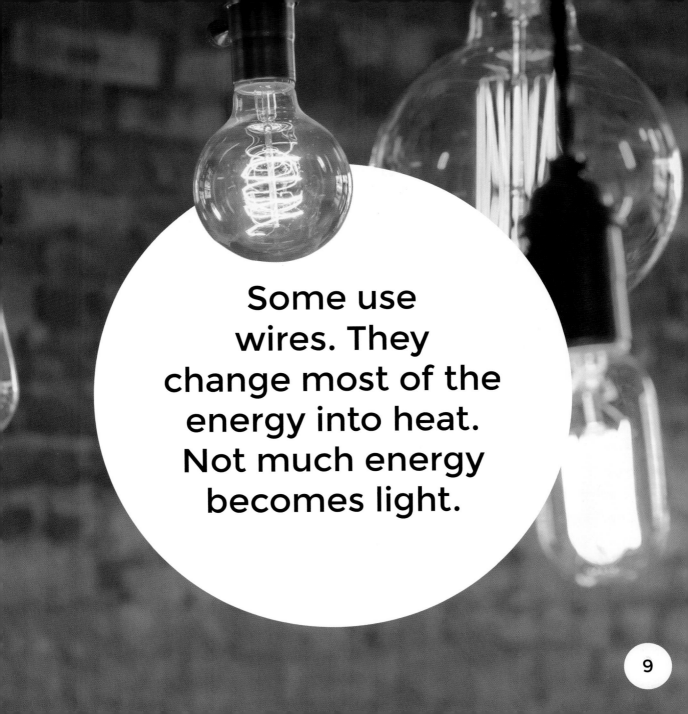

Some use wires. They change most of the energy into heat. Not much energy becomes light.

Other lightbulbs use gas.
They turn more energy into light.

Less energy becomes heat.
Using these lightbulbs
conserves energy.

Engineering

Green roofs reuse rainwater.
Grass and plants grow
on the roofs.

Layers of fabric help soil
soak up water. This helps
the water not be wasted.

Art

One artist made an **app.**
Users grew **digital** trees.

The trees showed on the
Eiffel Tower. Then a real tree
was planted for each user.

Math

People do about 215 loads of dishes each year. Many wash dishes by hand. But an average dishwasher uses about 15 gallons (57 L) less water in each load. It saves water.

Showers help conserve
water, too. A bath uses about
70 gallons (265 L) of water.

A shower
uses much
less.

19

Key Stats

- The United States uses more energy than any other country.

- Many people cut down forests in the 1800s. The US government created national parks in part to protect them.

- The International Union for Conservation of Nature (IUCN) was formed in 1948. It works with local people to protect animal species.

Glossary

app - short for application, a program on an electronic device.

digital - something made with computer technology.

energy - power that can be used to do work.

natural resource - a material produced by the earth that is useful to people. Forests, water, oil, and minerals are natural resources.

protecting - keeping something safe from injury or harm.

Booklinks

For more information
on conservation, please visit
booklinks.abdopublishing.com

Learn even more with the Abdo Zoom
STEAM database. Check out
abdozoom.com for more information.

Index

artist, 14

dishes, 16

Eiffel Tower, 15
energy, 8, 9, 10, 11

green roofs, 12

heat, 9, 11

light, 8, 9, 10
lightbulbs, 8, 10

natural
  resources, 4

plants, 12, 15

water, 12, 13, 16, 18